Foreword

Most of Earth was a frontier to Europeans in the 18th century, as uncharted and mysterious as another planet. British captain James Cook commanded three exploratory voyages of Earth's unknown oceans and far-flung islands —indeed, his first vessel, *Endeavour*, discovered the "unknown land of the south" now called Australia.

A ship's crew typically included professional sailors and builders, as well as ne'er-do-wells and delinquents—such as young Nick—forced into service. The *Endeavour* also carried a variety of scientists and artists to document the plants, animals, people, and places the *Endeavour* encountered. Of the 94 crew members who set sail, a third died on the voyage.

This journal of Nicholas Young is inspired by those kept by Cook and his scientists, which noted very little about the youngest sailor beyond these facts: his name and likely age; that one of his duties was caring for the ship's milk goat, Navy (which had already sailed widely on a previous voyage); and that he was first to sight both New Zealand and—after 2 years, 10 months, and 23 days at sea—the English coast. Nothing is known of Nick's life beyond this voyage.

written by Michael J. Rosen

illustrated by Maria Cristina Pritelli

Creative Editions

Sailing the Unknown

Around the World with Captain Cook

19 August 1768, Plymouth

Once there's a fair Wind,

Endeavour will leave England for a Continent

None has mapped — None knows exists.

She will not return soon — if She returns.

If Someone finds this Journal

my Name was Nicholas Young,

11 Years of Age.

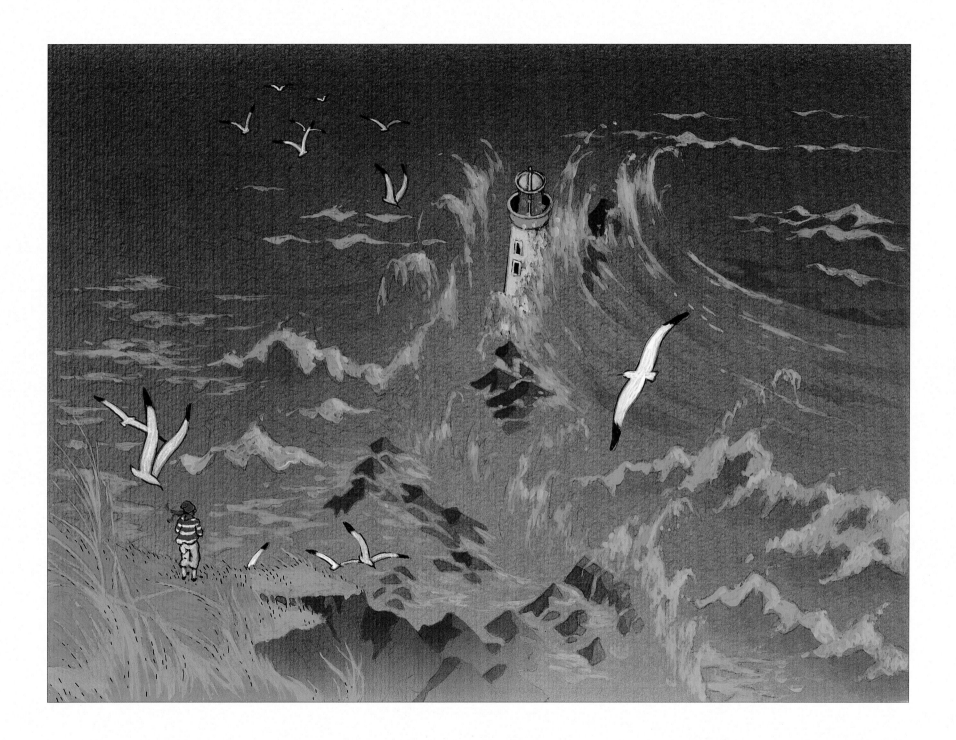

We are 93 Voices from England's every Corner—
plus 1 from the American Colonies.

Captain Cook and his Officers.
Scientists and Painters and their Servants and Dogs—
Theirs is the Upper Deck.
We Rogues forced to sail are below with the 16 Marines.
I am the smallest—just taller than Navy, the Goat.

25 August 1768, Day 1

We weighed Anchor—Gulls drowned out Farewells.

First Winds filled Endeavour's Sails. Ropes squeaked. Timbers groaned.
Providence sends the Breezes, but She sails by our Sweat.

Day 7, North Atlantic

Four hours heaving—Endeavour shook like Gambling Dice:
one Boat and Cages of Hens—all overboard!
She is seaworthy, but We are seasick.

Day 15

Stifling Heat! None can sleep but Navy.
None can be happy but the Rats and Cockroaches.

Day 21

Rope Burns, Lice, Salt crusting on my Face!
Frayed Ropes are our Napkins—so greasy
they light like Candles, the Light by which I write Here.

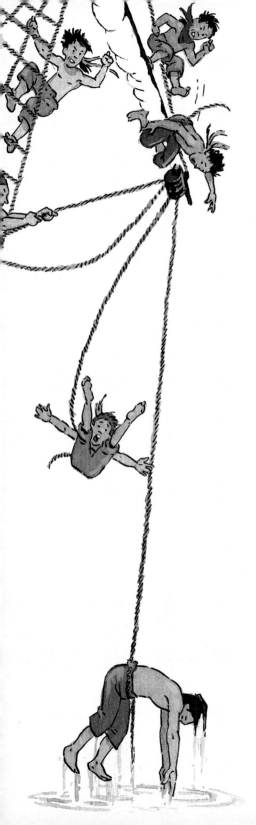

Day 29, Canary Islands

Months from Shore—yet Swallows still reach Us?
Through a Porthole—a Fish that flies!

Day 61, The Equator

Nighttime now matches Daytime to the Minute.

Seafarers' Tradition: All who had not before crossed the Equator
were thrice dunked! Tied fast to the Block, hoisted high—
plunged—and yanked up, choking for air.

Singing and Drinking all Night.

Day 96, Rio de Janeiro

With each Degree of Latitude We drop,
Temperature drops. But the Sea's Violence rises.
It is Summer—yet Snow blankets this Southern World.

Day 126

Sailors sing, Shipmen bark, Scientists lecture—
only Waves and Navy hear Me.
Neither answers Yes nor No to keep Me company.

Day 139, Tierra del Fuego, Land of Fire

Strange People. They wear not even Fig Leaves for
Modesty or Warmth! Yet They survive this Cold—
their Fires ever burning.

Day 151

Howling Squalls and Snow—Endeavour is a Bottle
tossing on angry Swells. We rope down Everything—
Thrice Captain cannot steer Her through the Straits.

Day 152, Cape Horn

Every Weight hauled below, at last She rounded the Cape—
the Gate between Oceans.

Day 190

Seas and Skies seem one—upside down, the View's the same.
Mists lift but reveal Nothing.
Hours repeat like the Marines' Drill,
marching back and forth, going Nowhere.

Depression envelops Endeavour.
Only the Cats and Rats don't feel It—They play Hide and Seek.

Navy gives but
little Milk.

*Tierra del Fuego,
Land of Fire*

*Angry Swells and bitter
Cold—We long to feel
the Fires of the Shore.*

Day 231, Tahiti

Land! Providence must invent It

just to keep the Lost from leaping overboard.

Day 275

We offer the Tahitians Beads, Clothes, Yarn—all Naught to Us.

They offer Coconuts, Fish, Breadfruit—all Naught to Them.

This would be Eden but for the Mosquitoes!

Even as one Artist paints, They eat his Pigments off the Paper.

Natives paint too—their Canvas is Skin.

They stab with Bones to stain the Flesh blue-black.

Tattoo They call this—*7* Mates now wear Them forever.

Day 298

Thieves! They stole Clothing, Rakes, Firearms, Portholes—
even our Lightning Rod!
Endeavour is their Treasure Chest to plunder.
Their Island is Ours.

Day 323

Every Landing, the Scientists collect new Specimens.
The Crew collects Provisions. Today we also leave with Tupia,
who knows these Islands and Languages.
Tayeto, his Servant, plays a Flute with his Nostril!

Day 375

So many sickened with Island Disease.
Chores are doubled, tripled.

All Hope is funneled into the Mate's Eyes atop the Masthead.
Captain will name the Coast for Him who spies It.

Day 407

Land! I saw It on my Watch! An Island? The Unknown Continent?
Chalky Cliffs, sandy Bays, green-blue Forests, violet Mountains.

Whoso voyages Here will know this Point as Young Nick's Head.

Day 409, New Zealand

We anchored—Maori Spears struck like Lightning Bolts.
We want only Fresh Water, not Fighting.

Day 411

Maori returned to Endeavour with Fish to trade but seized Tayeto!
The Marines fired—the Warriors' Canoes scattered, Tayeto saved.

Captain named this place Cape Kidnappers.
Endless Land yet to Explore.

Day 525

Canoes—100 Warriors in each—stomp and chant.
On land, They dance with Limbs like Snakes—Tongues like Snakes.

A Boy my age, Te Horeta, pressed his Nose to mine—to Tayeto's.
Maori Greeting!
I shook his Hand in English Greeting.
From 3 Lands, the same Laughing.

The rest was Misunderstanding! Maori made Stew
to eat of Potatoes and our Candles and Shoes!
Even stranger—We learned They are Cannibals.
They eat Foes slain in Battle!

Day 574

Natives want Us gone. They told Tupia We are Demons:

—Our white Faces prove us Ghosts.

—We arrived on a giant Bird with white Wings.

—We row backward Boats and see behind us without Eyes.

—And what People have no Women?

Day 585

Six Months of Food remains as We depart—

if each Man starves a bit more.

Quarrels—not Captain—rule Endeavour.

Half side with the Scientists for more Exploration.

Half sigh only for Home and Roast Beef.

Day 602

Winds write a new Mystery—They pinch the Sea,

as if between Fingers, swirling Water Columns skyward.

The Spouts swell and vanish—then only Seabirds.

Endeavour is their Mystery.

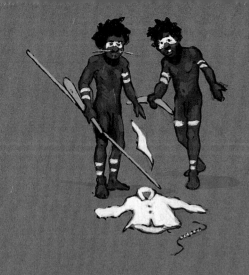

Day 603, Terra Australis Incognita, The Unknown Land of the South

Zachary sighted what None from England has seen—

endless Hills, Beaches, Capes. Captain gave English names to Each.

Day 604

Landed at a Beach clustered with Huts.

Warriors threatened with Lances while their People hid.

Even as the Captain's Nephew set foot—the 1st on Terra Australis—

1st Boots, not Feet—their Darts and Stones rained upon Us.

Day 608

They will not trade—not for Nails, Ribbons, Anything.

No one knows how to ask, What do You want, People?

But We know their Answer—Go away.

Day 611, Botany Bay

Endless Specimens for the Scientists!

Cockatoos, Lorikeets, Oysters, Crabs,

Creatures who breathe both air and water.

And an 80-pound leaping Mouse that   outraces even our Greyhound!

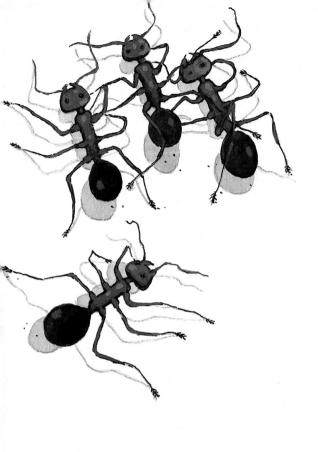

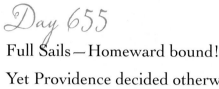

Day 655

Full Sails—Homeward bound!

Yet Providence decided otherwise—a Reef shatters our Hull.

Breaking Timbers echo in the Waves that flood Us.

Pumps cannot keep up. Firewood, Cannons—

All is thrown overboard! Still the Water onboard anchors Us.

Day 656

Every Man tugging, She struggled free.

Still We sank!—until one Mate thought to drag a Sail beneath Her Hull.

The Sea plugged the Bandage inward, saving Us.

Day 658

Now We repair in this inhospitable Land

of biting Ants, stinging Caterpillars, fierce Mosquitoes.

Day 721

Seaworthy again, empty Barrels lashed everywhere for Buoyancy —
We attempt our Escape yet Endeavour hurls toward the Reef's 8-foot Teeth.
Nearly too late, Providence sends Winds that save Us from the Watery Inferno.
Endeavour will not be Pieces of the Reef's Collection.

Day 730

We hoisted the English Colors, leaving this Continent
claimed now for King George III.

Day 761

Homesickness reshapes Clouds into Signs of Land.

Day 831, Batavia, Java

Months repairing again — Worms have rotted the Keel.
Fever spreads its Wildfire among Us.
Malaria claims first Tayeto, my Friend.

Day 834

Now Tupia lost! His Languages, his Travels—lost, too.

Day 852

Our third Christmas at sea—but We have no glad Tidings.

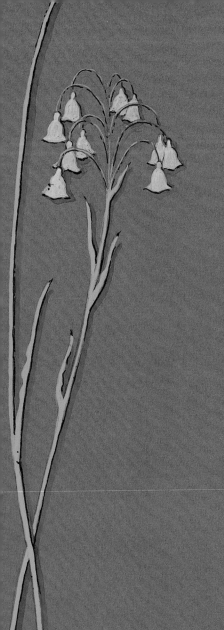

Day 868, Prince's Island

A new Disease boarded along with the Fruit and Water.
Today, there are but 9 to sail Endeavour—We are a floating Hospital.

Day 928, Cape Town, South Africa

Another Continent, with still stranger Species—
Serpent-necked Ostriches, striped Horses, Cassowaries—
Earth yet holds Creatures that are Nothing like Anything else!

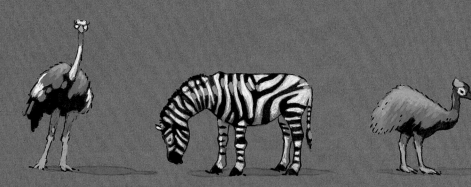

Day 1,046

A Brig flying English Colors brings last year's Newspaper—
"Endeavour sunk! All perished!" We must be a Ghost Ship.

Day 1,056

Land! I cried from the Masthead—Home!
But England is now the Unknown Land to Me.
Nearly 14, I have seen more of Earth than Anyone
excepting my Shipmates—excepting Navy, Who has twice our Travels.

Forty thousand Miles later—Endeavour, too,
returned a different Ship—
Her Skin of Hull, Lungs of Sails, Spine of Mast, Muscles of Rope—
Surgeons in every Port replaced Them.

We brought home 1,400 strange Creatures,
gave unknown Lands new English Names,
and opened a new World for Colonies.

29 July 1771

Home for mere Days, Some sign on for another Voyage.

Not Young Nick. Not Navy. Ah, my Goat.

She lived but Weeks after our Landing—

Her Voyages by Sea complete. As are Mine.

Nicholas Young

Text copyright © 2012 Michael J. Rosen

Illustrations copyright © 2012 Maria Cristina Pritelli

Published in 2012 by Creative Editions

P.O. Box 227, Mankato, MN 56002 USA

Creative Editions is an imprint of The Creative Company

Edited by Aaron Frisch

Designed by Rita Marshall

Printed in Italy

Library of Congress Cataloging-in-Publication Data

Rosen, Michael J., 1954–

Sailing the unknown: around the world with captain Cook /

written by Michael J. Rosen; illustrated by Maria Cristina Pritelli.

Summary: A sailor boy named Nick travels the uncharted world of the
late 1700s in this illustrated account of the historic three-year voyage
of the British vessel *Endeavour* and its captain, James Cook.

ISBN 978-1-56846-216-5

[1. Voyages around the world—Fiction. 2. Cook, James, 1728–1779—Fiction.
3. Explorers—Fiction. 4. Sea stories. 5. Diaries—Fiction.]

I. Pritelli, Maria Cristina, ill. II. Title.

PZ7.R71868Sai 2012   [Fic]—dc23   2011040840

First edition

2 4 6 8 9 7 5 3 1